THIS BOOK BELONGS TO...

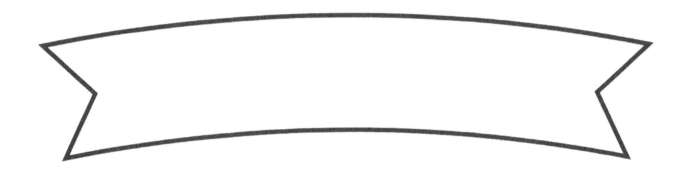

TABLE OF CONTENTS

INTRODUCTION

A little bit of history...

Japanese is an East Asian language spoken by about 128 million people, primarly in Japan, where its the national language. Little is known of the language's prehistory or when it first appeared in Japan. Chinese documents from the 3rd century recorded a few Japanese words, but substantial texts did not appear until the 8th century.

In Japanese, « Japanese language » is said « nihongo » (日本語). The characters 日本 means Japan and the last character, 語, means language. However, the Japanese themselves use the word kokugo (国語, « language of the country » or « national language ») to refer to their language.

Why is there two basic writing systems ?

Hiragana are usually used for particles, words and parts of words.
Katakana are usually used for foreign words and names, loan words and most country names. Katakana makes it easier for Japanese people to pronounce foreign words. It is also used to write onomatopoeisa sounds like you would see in Japanese mangas.

There is a third type of Japanese letters : Kanji, which are adopted logographic Chinese characters. They are usually used for the stem of words and to convey the meaning as well as sound.

Where should i start my learning journey?

It is highly suggested to start with learning Hiragana, then Katakana and finish with Kanji. That's the way it is done in Japanese schools.
Why ? Because if you learn Hiragana first and then Katakana you will become familiar with all the Japanese sounds that are permitted (vowels, consonants, longs vowels and long consonants). You will be able to read native Japanese resources written by Japanese for Japanese people and it will be easier to learn Kanji atferwards.

HIRAGANA CHART

a	i	u	e	o	
あ	い	う	え	お	
ka	ki	ku	ke	ko	
か	き	く	け	こ	
sa	shi	su	se	so	
さ	し	す	せ	そ	
ta	chi	tsu	te	to	
た	ち	つ	て	と	
na	ni	nu	ne	no	
な	に	ぬ	ね	の	
ha	hi	fu	he	ho	
は	ひ	ふ	へ	ほ	
ma	mi	mu	me	mo	
ま	み	む	め	も	
ya		yu		yo	
や		ゆ		よ	
ra	ri	ru	re	ro	
ら	り	る	れ	ろ	
wa				wo	-n
わ				を	ん

KATAKANA CHART

a	i	u	e	o	
ア	イ	ウ	エ	オ	
ka	ki	ku	ke	ko	
カ	キ	ク	ケ	コ	
sa	shi	su	se	so	
サ	シ	ス	セ	ソ	
ta	chi	tsu	ta	to	
タ	チ	ツ	テ	ト	
na	ni	nu	ne	no	
ナ	ニ	ヌ	ネ	ノ	
ha	hi	fu	he	ho	
ハ	ヒ	フ	ヘ	ホ	
ma	mi	mu	me	mo	
マ	ミ	ム	メ	モ	
ya		yu		yo	
ヤ		ユ		ヨ	
ra	ri	ru	re	ro	
ラ	リ	ル	レ	ロ	
wa				wo	-n
ワ				ヲ	ン

ga	za	da	ba	pa
が	ざ	だ	ば	ぱ
gi	ji	dji	bi	pi
ぎ	じ	ぢ	び	ぴ
gu	zu	dzu	bu	pu
ぐ	ず	づ	ぶ	ぷ
ge	ze	de	be	pe
げ	ぜ	で	べ	ぺ
go	zo	do	bo	po
ご	ぞ	ど	ぼ	ぽ

kya	kyu	kyo
きゃ	きゅ	きょ
gya	gyu	gyo
ぎゃ	ぎゅ	ぎょ
sha	shu	sho
しゃ	しゅ	しょ
ja	ju	jo
じゃ	じゅ	じょ
cha	chu	cho
ちゃ	ちゅ	ちょ
nya	nyu	nyo
にゃ	にゅ	にょ
hya	hyu	hyo
ひゃ	ひゅ	ひょ
bya	byu	byo
びゃ	びゅ	びょ
pya	pyu	pyo
ぴゃ	ぴゅ	ぴょ
mya	myu	myo
みゃ	みゅ	みょ
rya	ryu	ryo
りゃ	りゅ	りょ

ga	za	da	ba	pa
ガ	ザ	ダ	バ	パ
gi	ji	ji	bi	pi
ギ	ジ	ヂ	ビ	ピ
gu	zu	dzu	bu	pu
グ	ズ	ヅ	ブ	プ
ge	ze	de	be	pe
ゲ	ゼ	デ	ベ	ペ
go	zo	do	bo	po
ゴ	ゾ	ド	ボ	ポ

kya	kyu	kyo
キャ	キュ	キョ
gya	gyu	gyo
ギャ	ギュ	ギョ
sha	shu	sho
シャ	シュ	ショ
ja	ju	jo
ジャ	ジュ	ジョ
cha	chu	cho
チャ	チュ	チョ
nya	nyu	nyo
ニャ	ニュ	ニョ
hya	hyu	hyo
ヒャ	ヒュ	ヒョ
bya	byu	byo
ビャ	ビュ	ビョ
pya	pyu	pyo
ピャ	ピュ	ピョ
mya	myu	myo
ミャ	ミュ	ミョ
rya	ryu	ryo
リャ	リュ	リョ

HIRAGANA

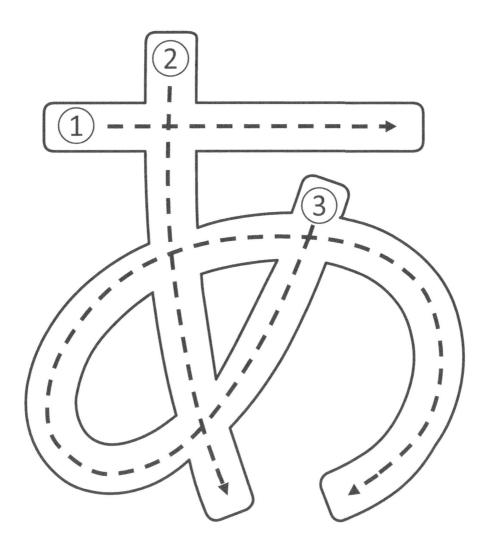

Should be pronounced « A »

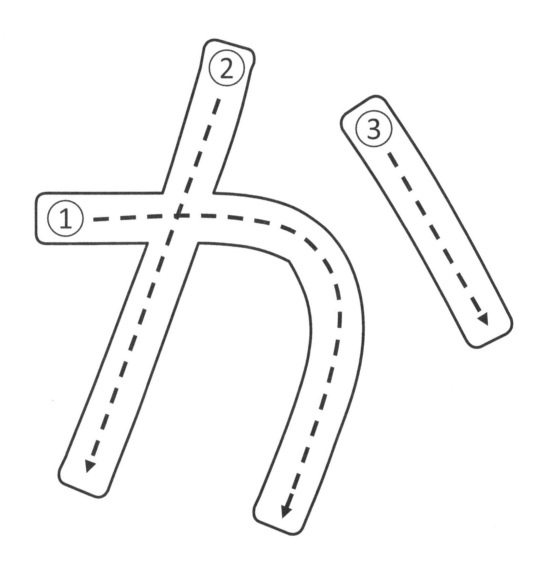

Should be pronounced « KA »

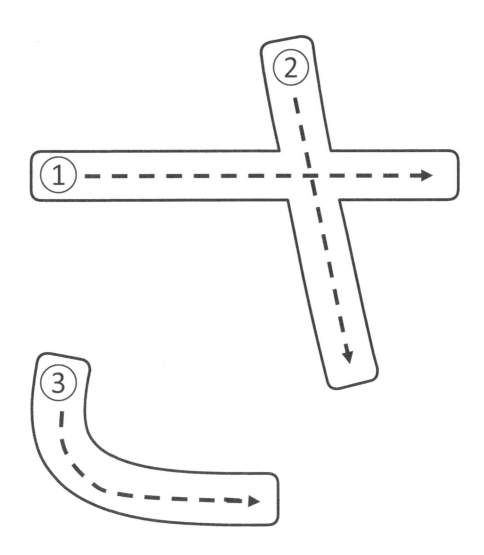

Should be pronounced « SA »

Should be pronounced « TA »

Should be pronounced « NA »

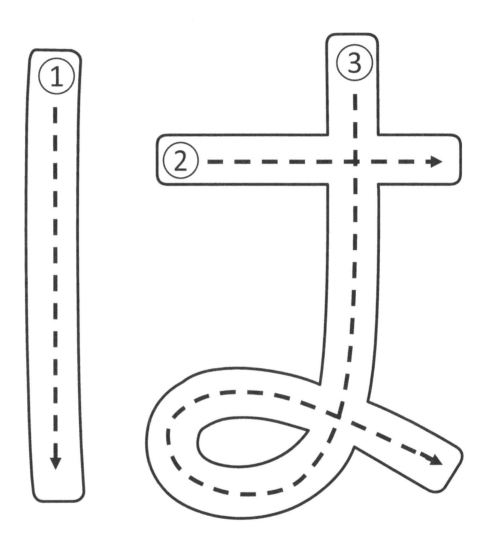

Should be pronounced « HA » (WA)

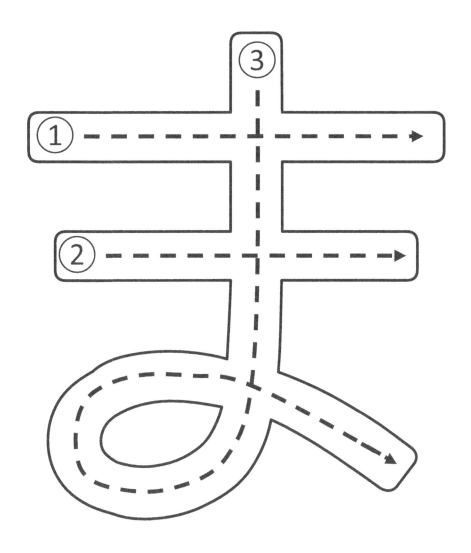

Should be pronounced « MA »

Should be pronounced « YA »

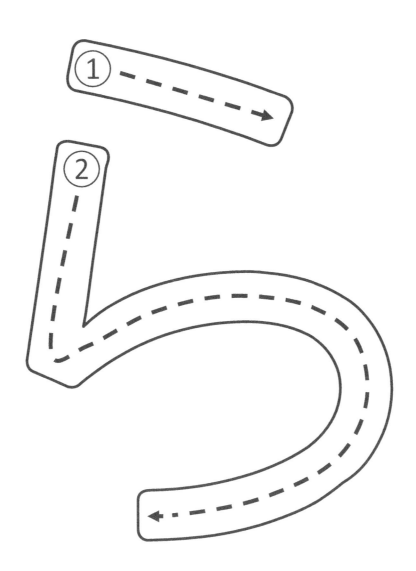

Should be pronounced « RA »

Should be pronounced « WA »

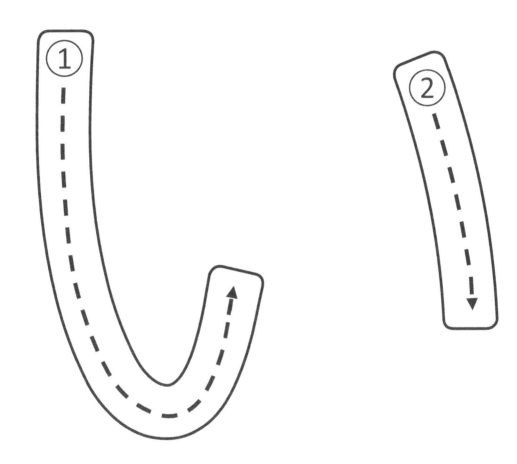

Should be pronounced « I »

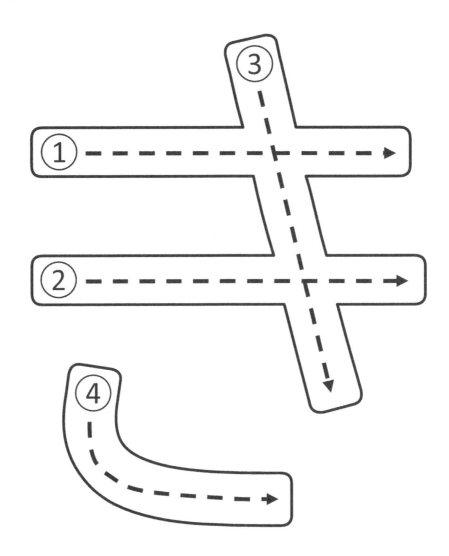

Should be pronounced « KI »

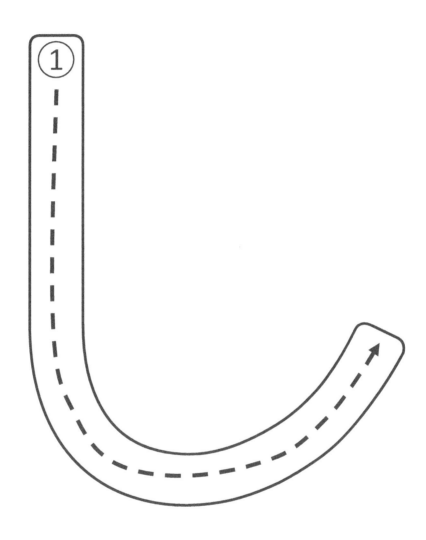

Should be pronounced « SHI »

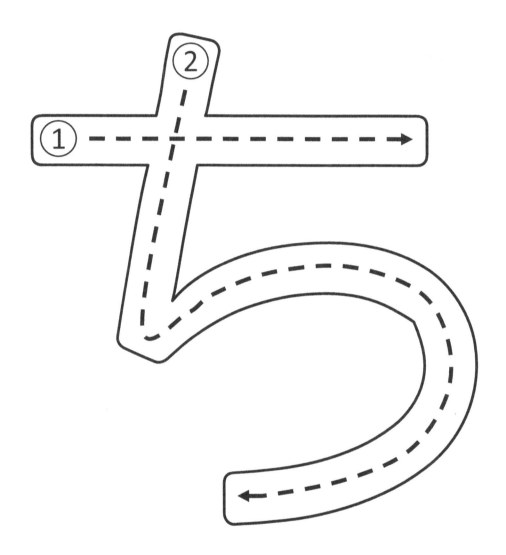

Should be pronounced « CHI »

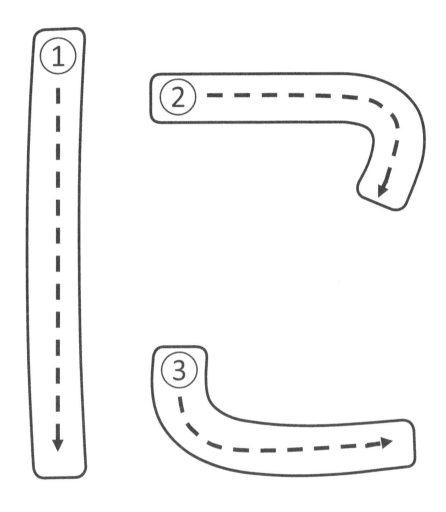

Should be pronounced « NI »

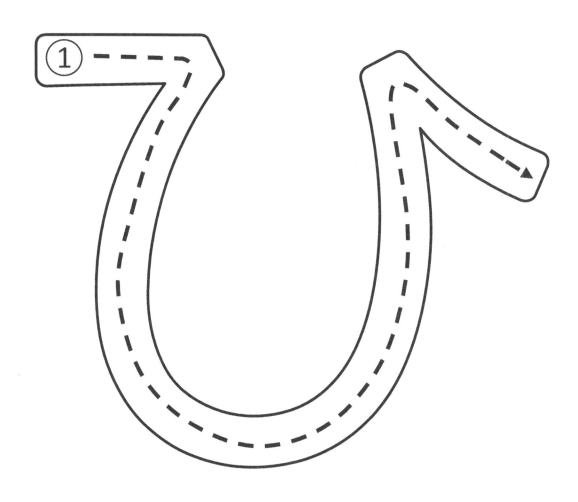

Should be pronounced « HI »

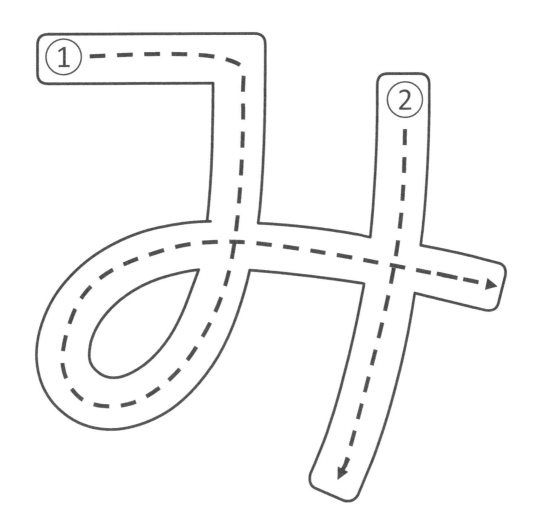

Should be pronounced « MI »

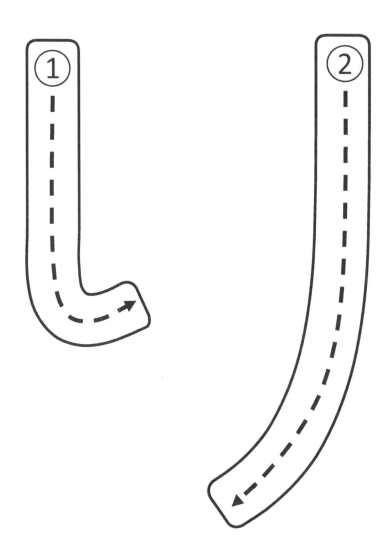

Should be pronounced « RI »

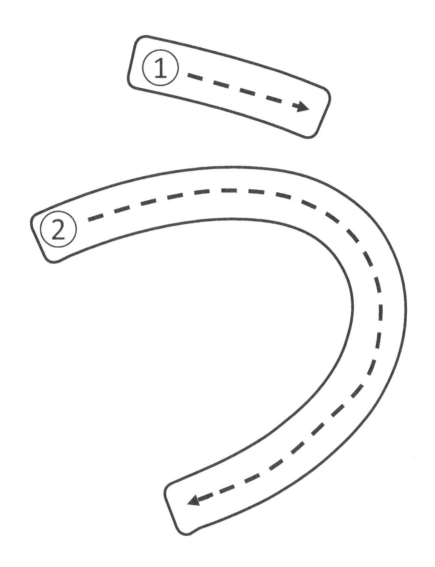

Should be pronounced « U »

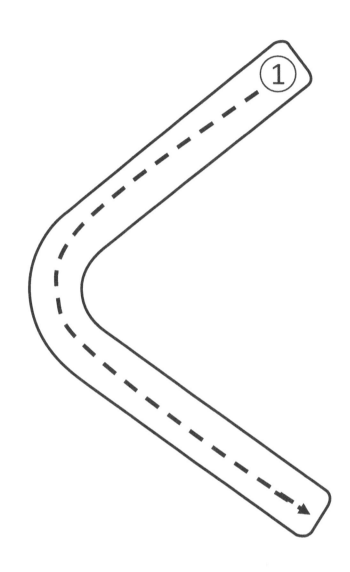

Should be pronounced « KU »

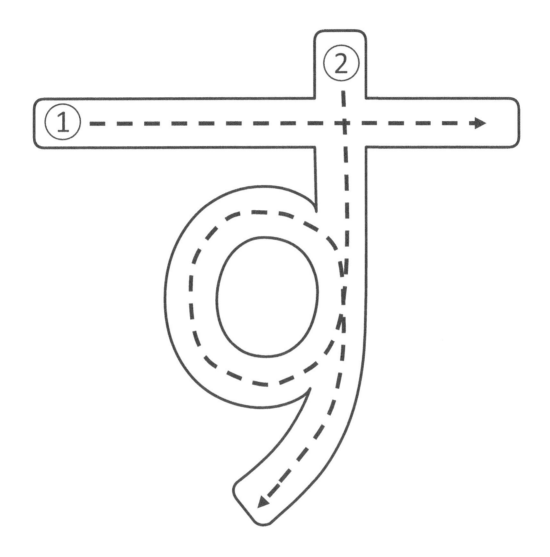

Should be pronounced « SU »

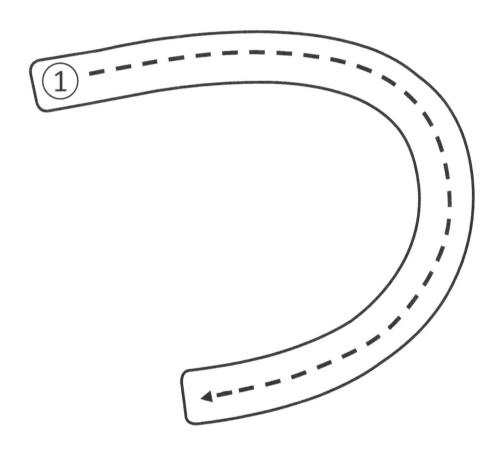

Should be pronounced « TSU »

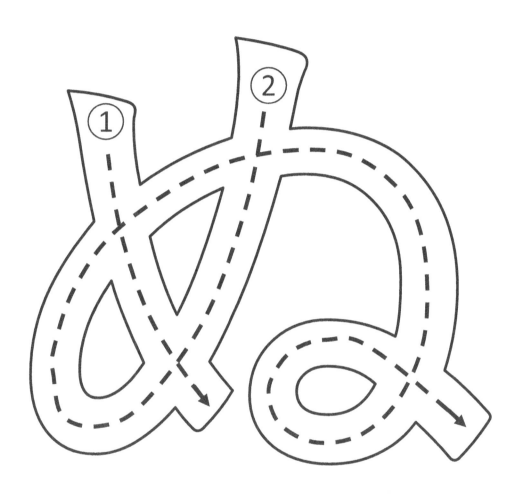

Should be pronounced « NU »

Should be pronounced « FU »

Should be pronounced « MU »

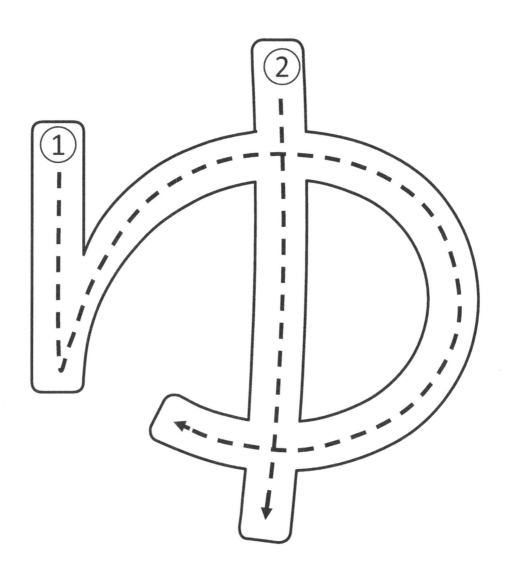

Should be pronounced « YU »

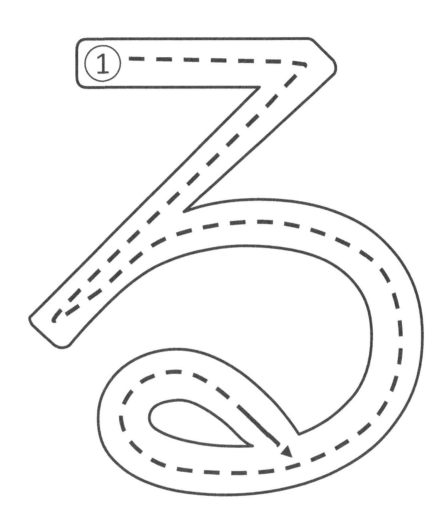

Should be pronounced « RU »

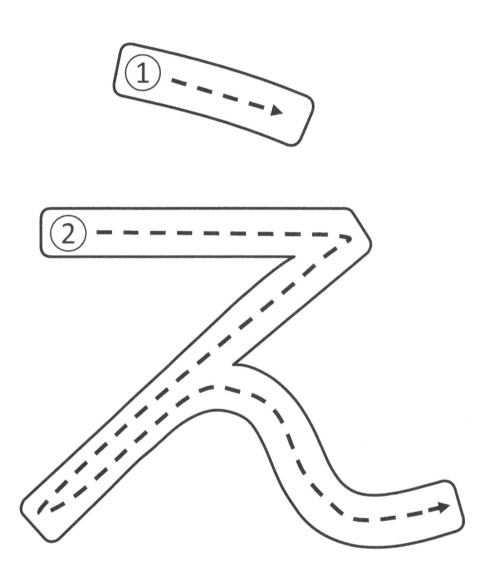

Should be pronounced « E »

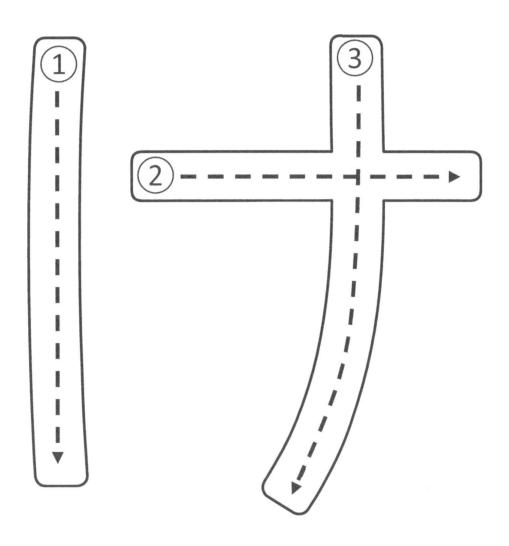

Should be pronounced « KE »

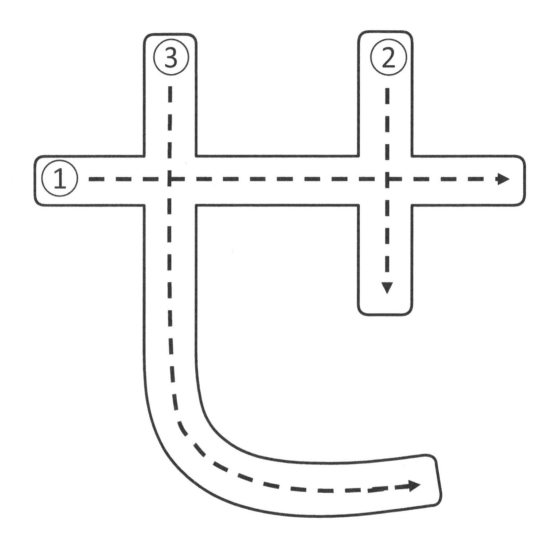

Should be pronounced « SE »

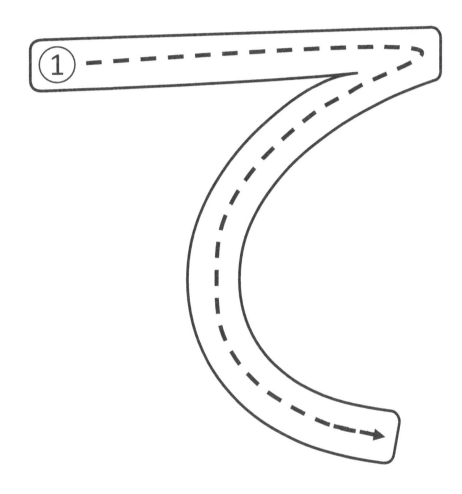

Should be pronounced « TE »

Should be pronounced « NE »

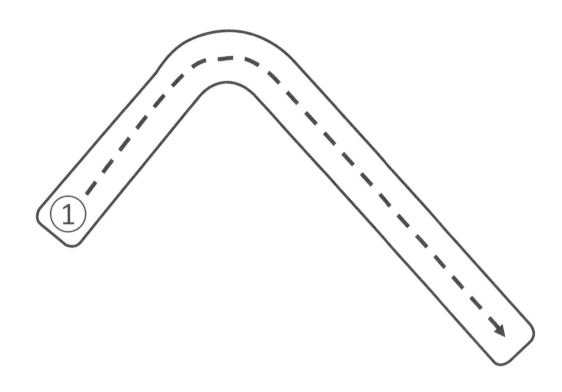

Should be pronounced « HE (E) »

Should be pronounced « ME »

Should be pronounced « RE »

Should be pronounced « O »

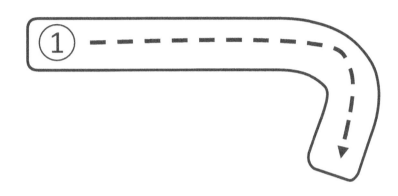

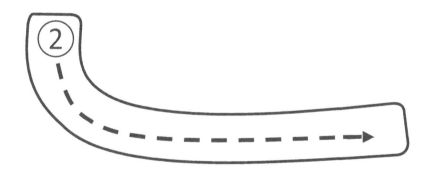

Should be pronounced « KO »

Should be pronounced « SO »

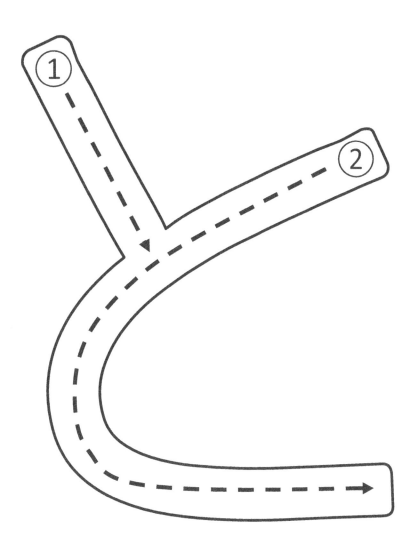

Should be pronounced « TO »

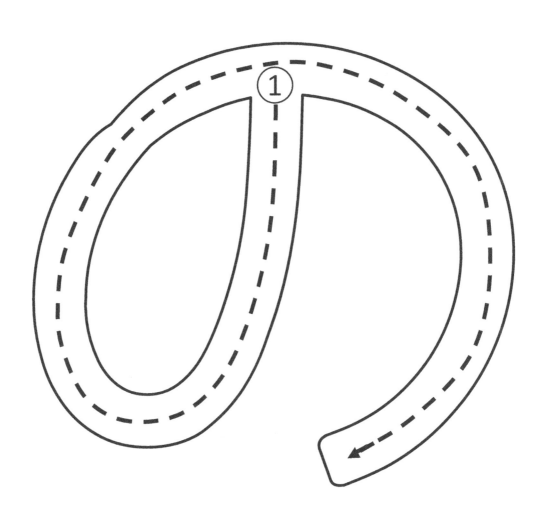

Should be pronounced « NO »

HIRAGANA – TRACE BIG CHARACTERS

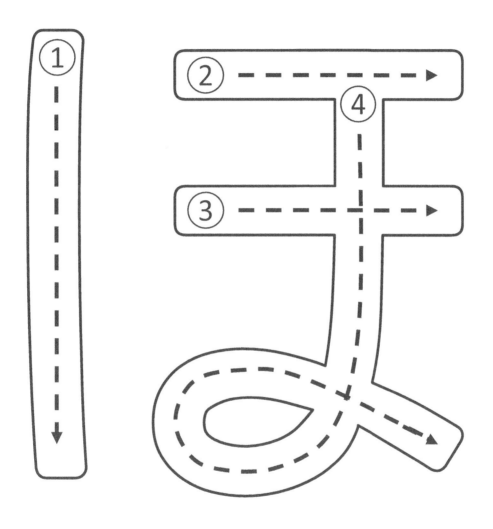

Should be pronounced « HO »

51

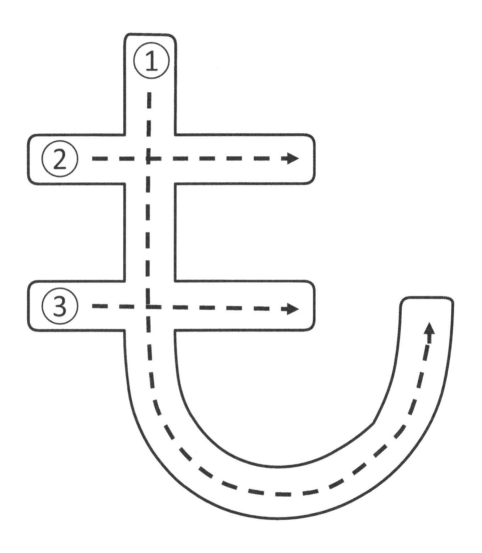

Should be pronounced « MO »

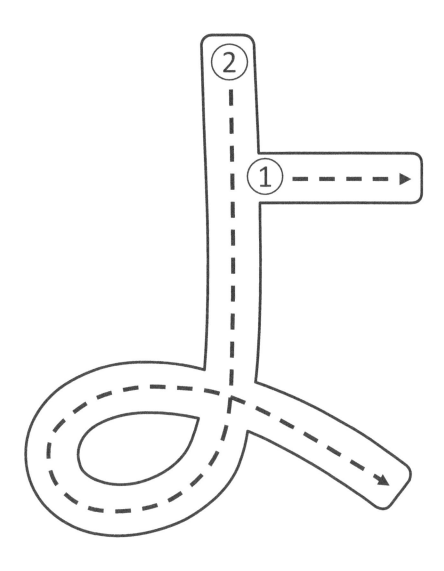

Should be pronounced « YO »

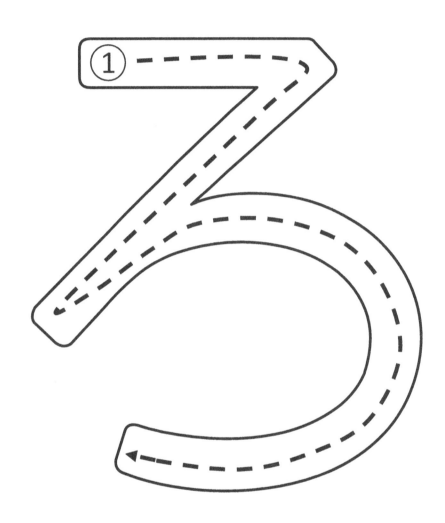

Should be pronounced « RO »

Should be pronounced « O* WO »

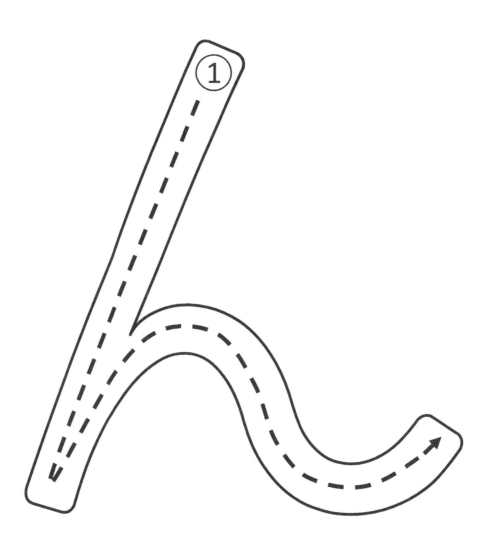

-N

HIRAGANA
SMALLER CHARACTERS

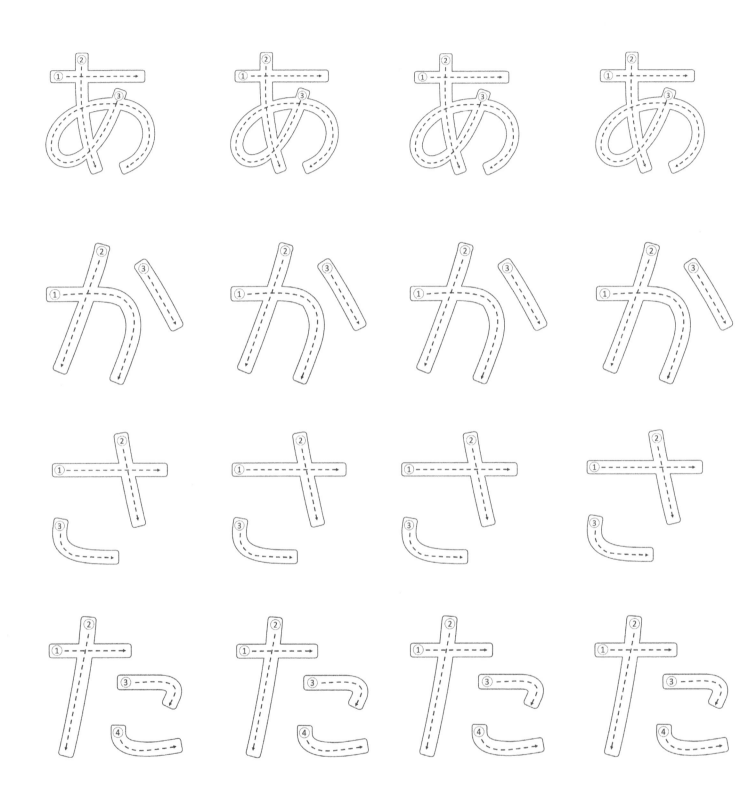

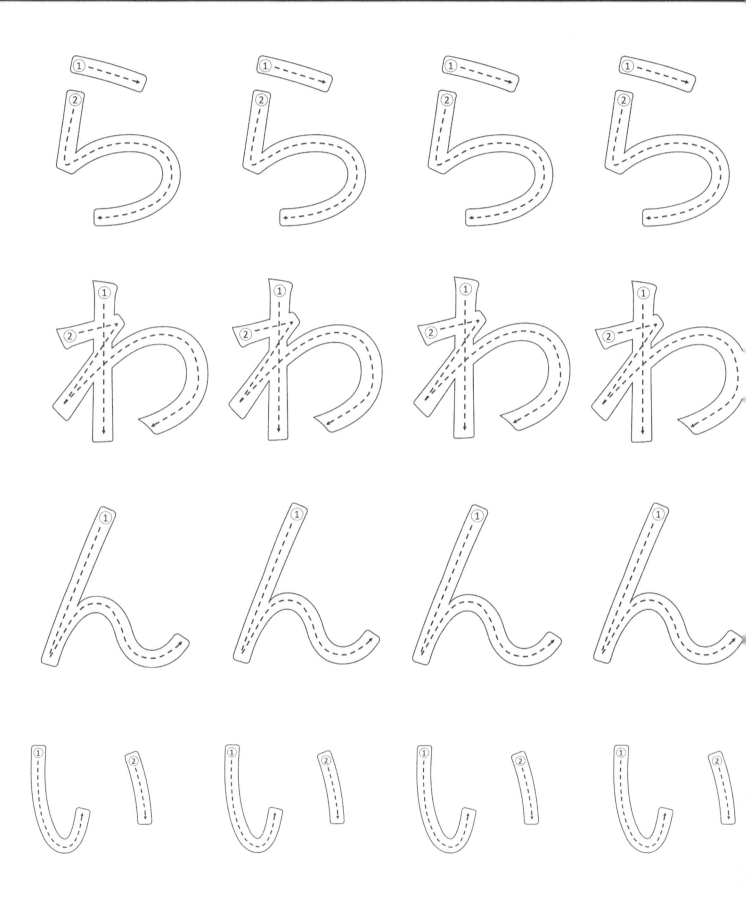

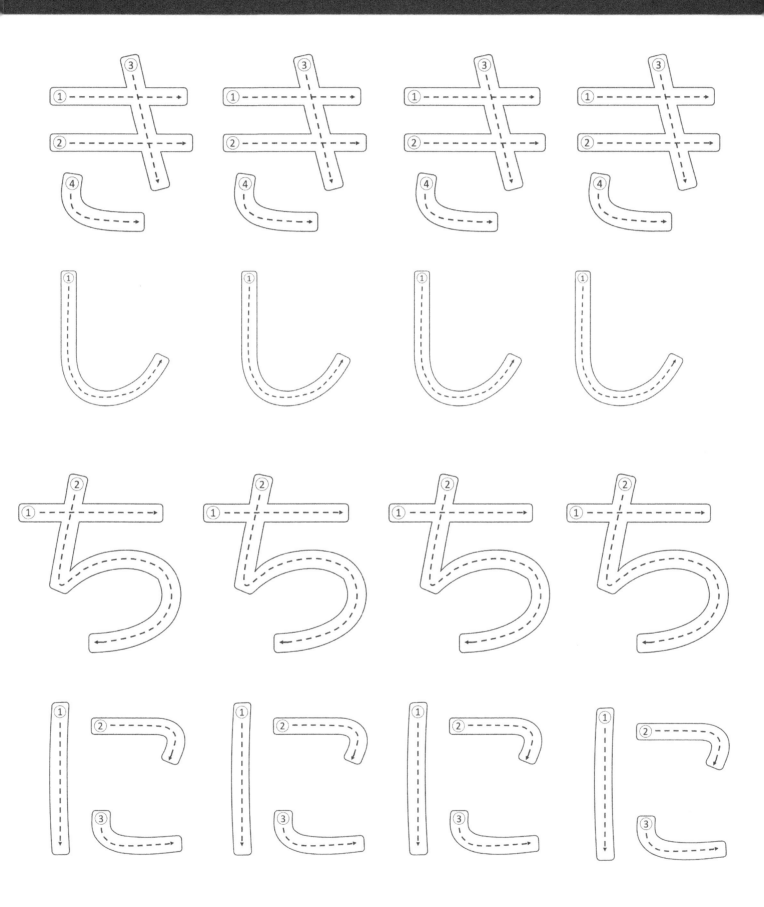

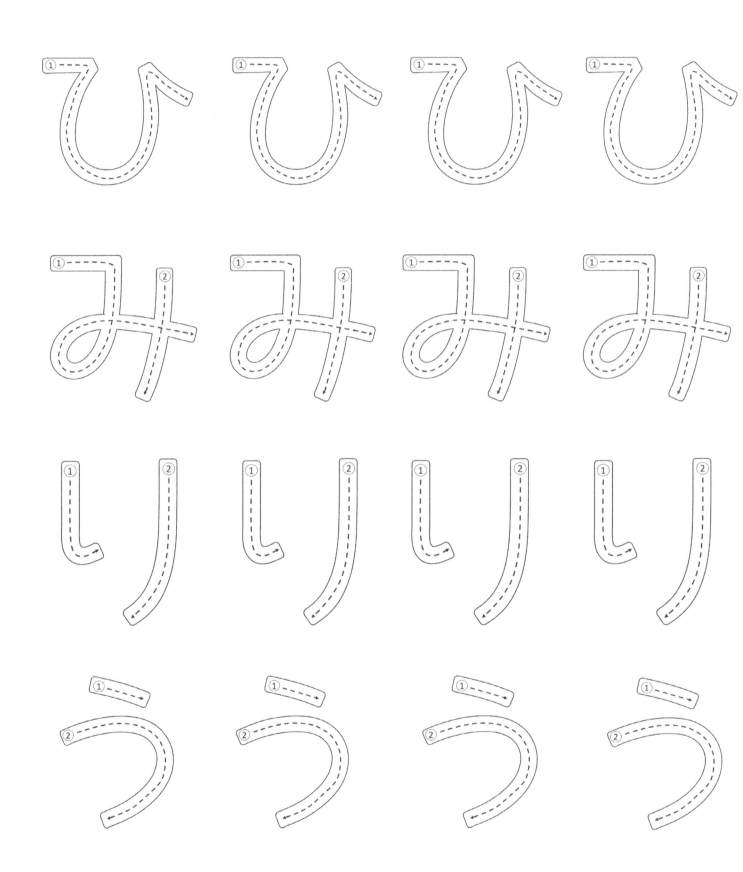

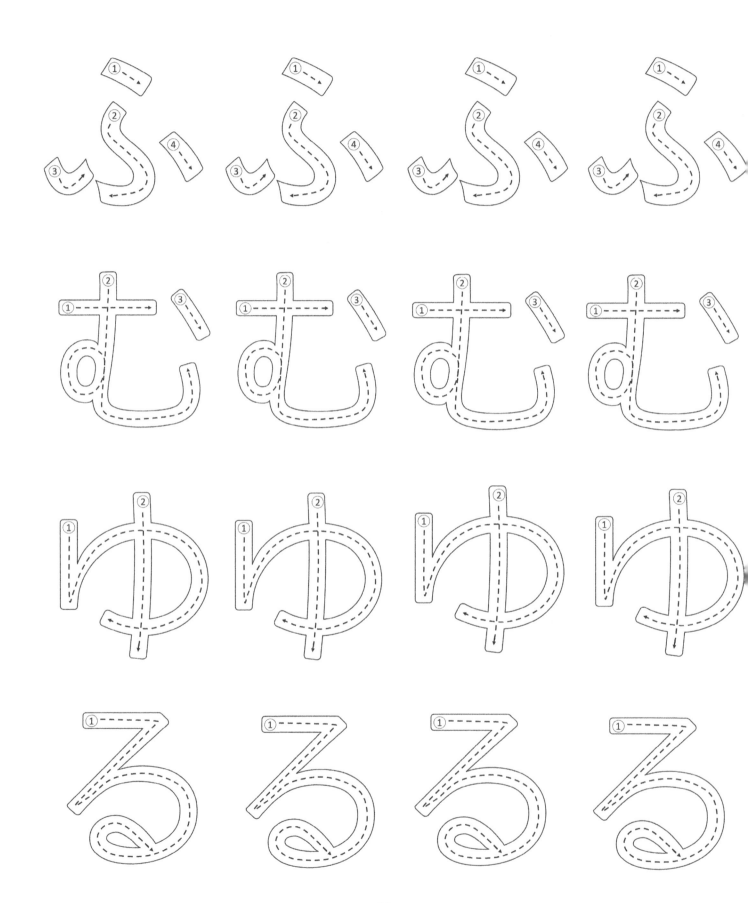

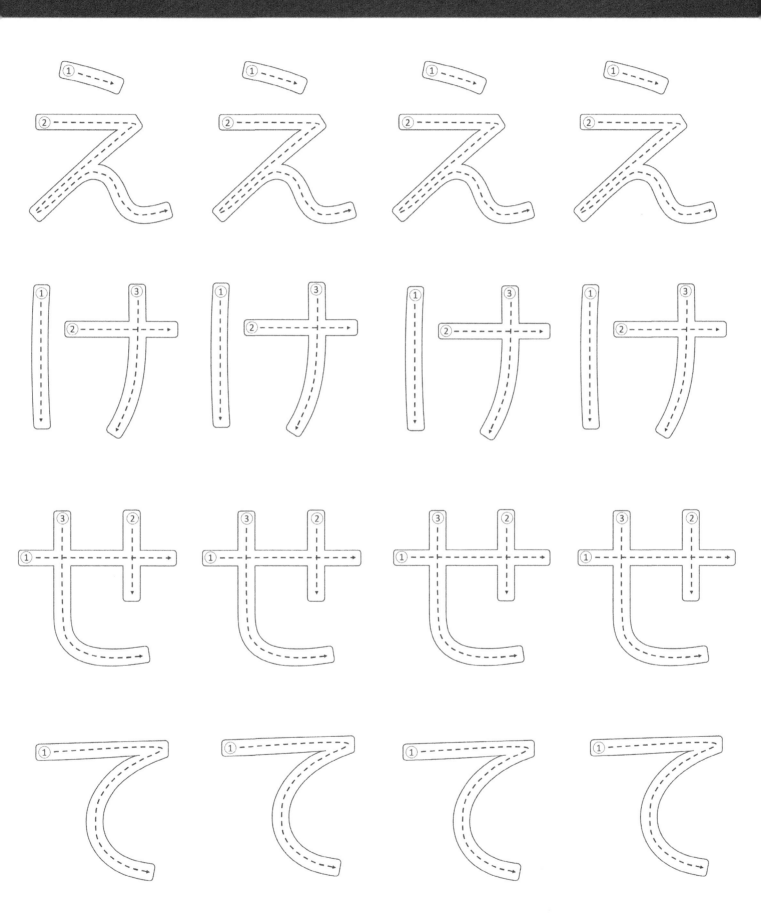

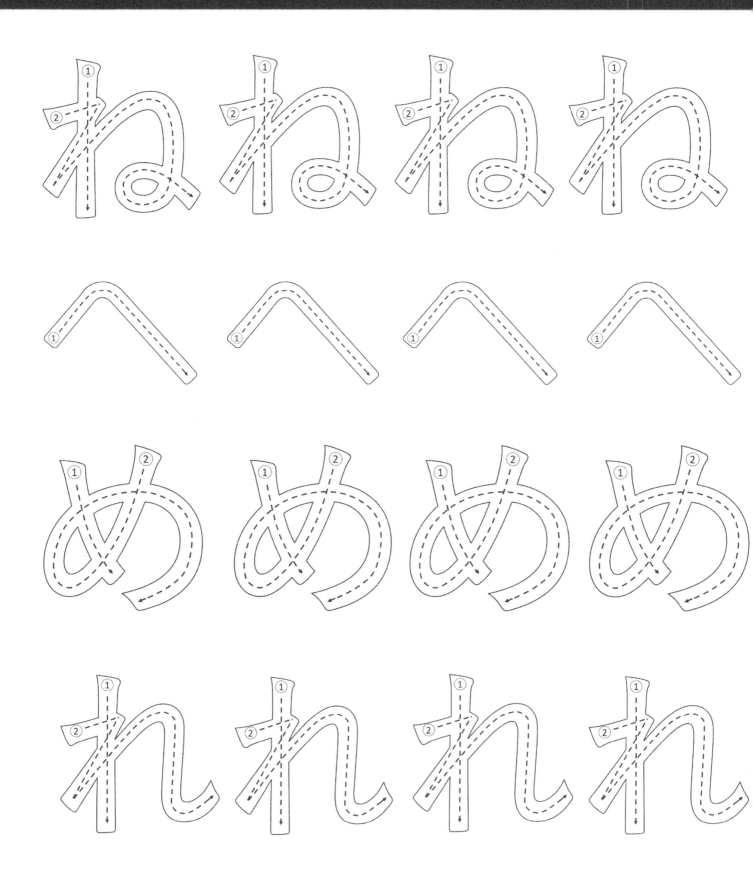

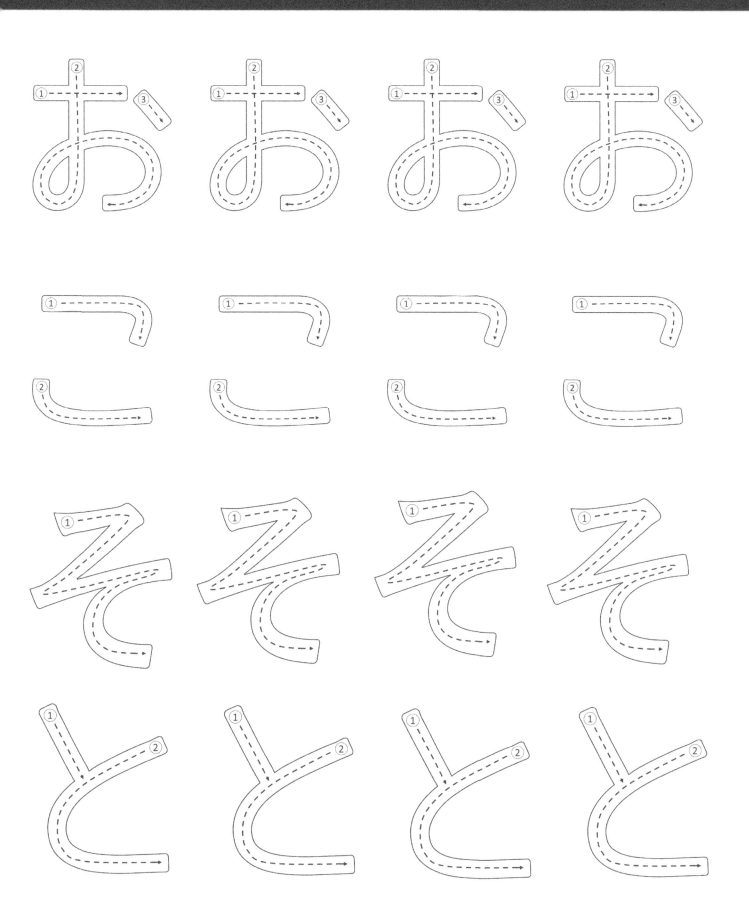

KATAKANA

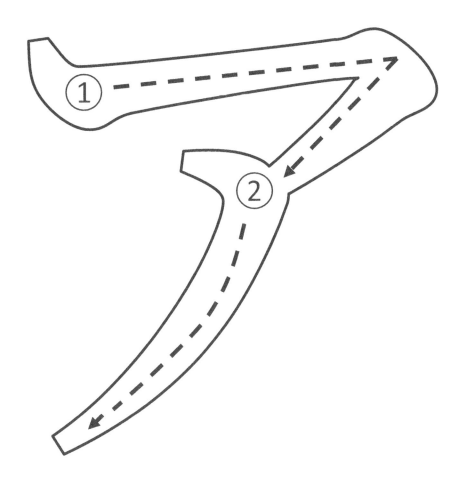

Should be pronounced « A »

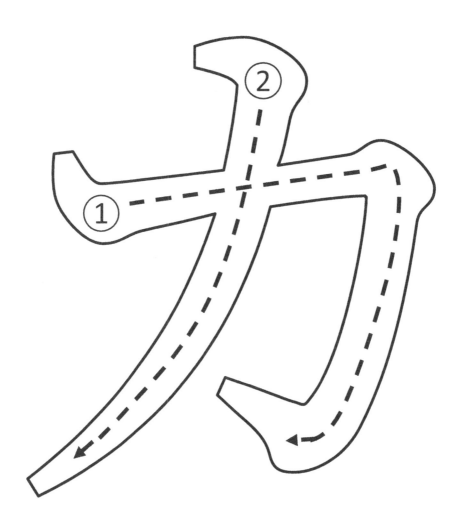

Should be pronounced « KA »

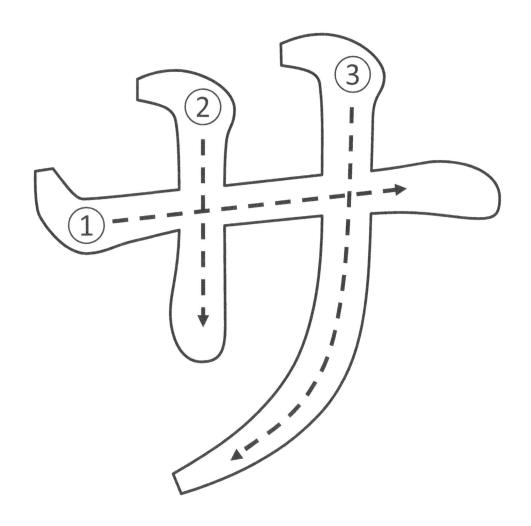

Should be pronounced « SA »

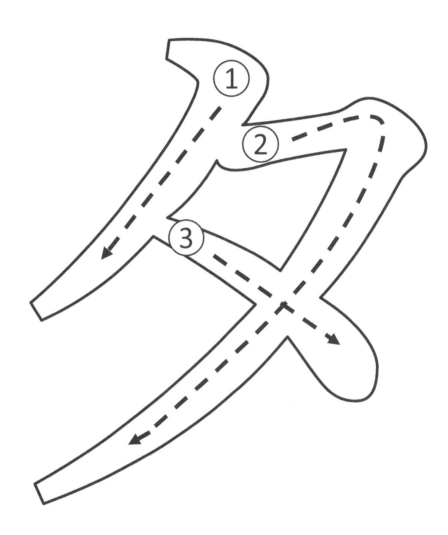

Should be pronounced « TA »

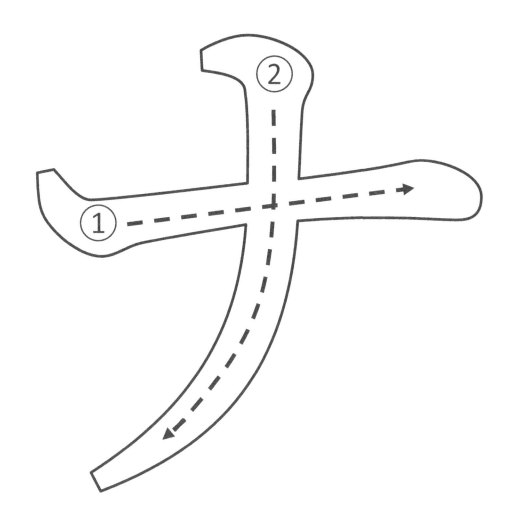

Should be pronounced « NA »

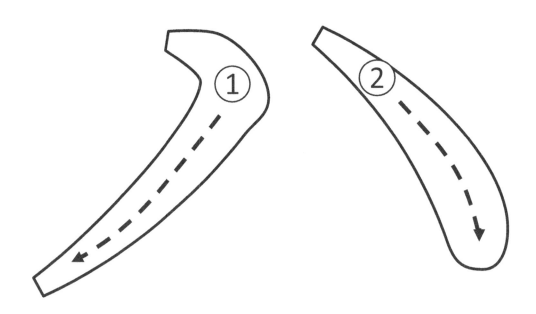

Should be pronounced « HA »

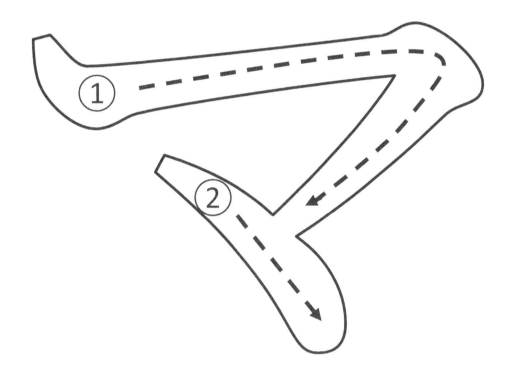

Should be pronounced « MA »

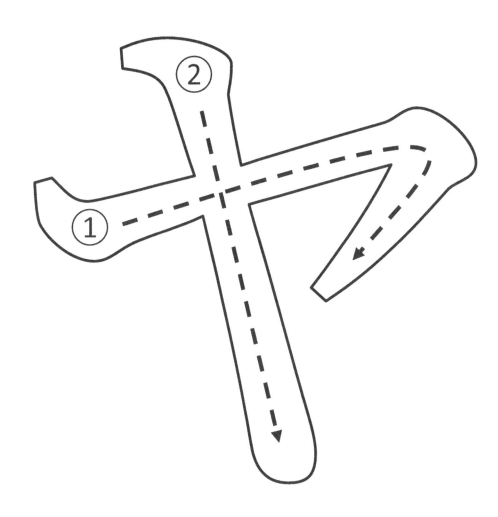

Should be pronounced « YA »

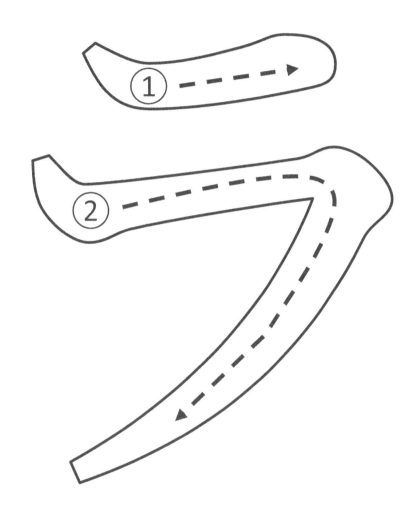

Should be pronounced « RA »

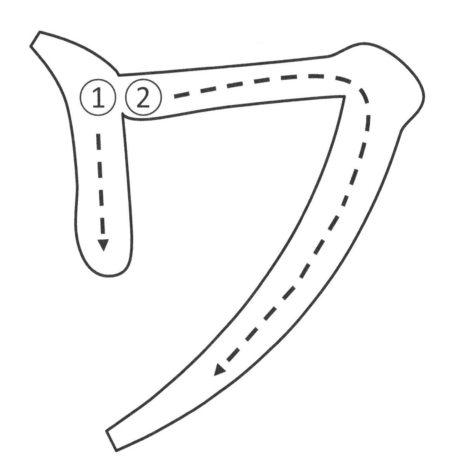

Should be pronounced « WA »

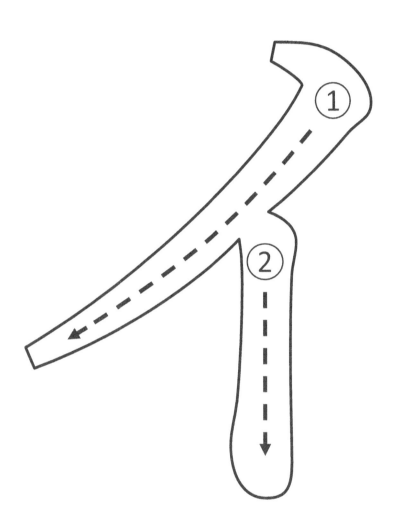

Should be pronounced « I »

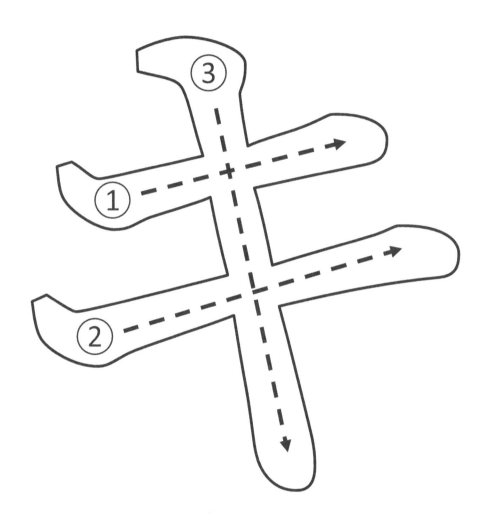

Should be pronounced « KI »

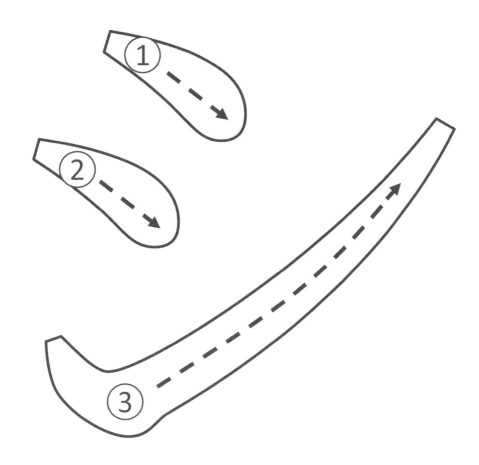

Should be pronounced « SHI »

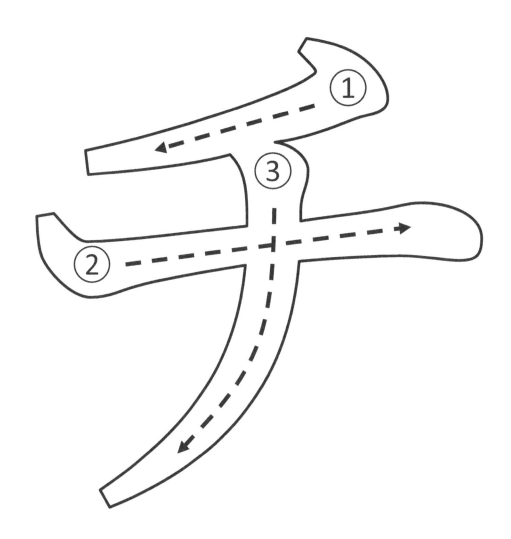

Should be pronounced « CHI »

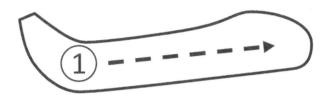

Should be pronounced « NI »

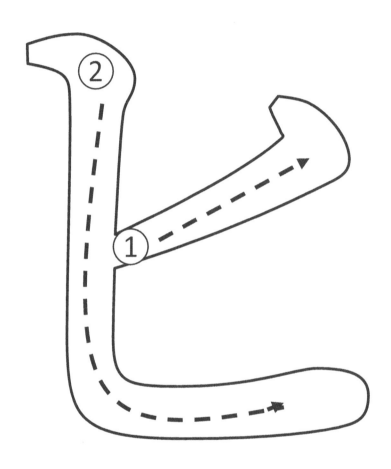

Should be pronounced « HI »

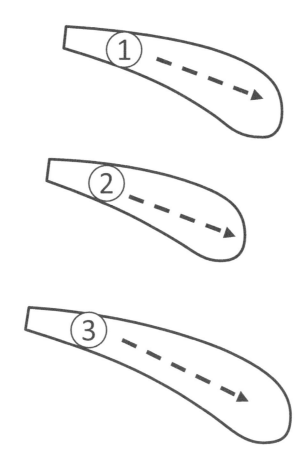

Should be pronounced « MI »

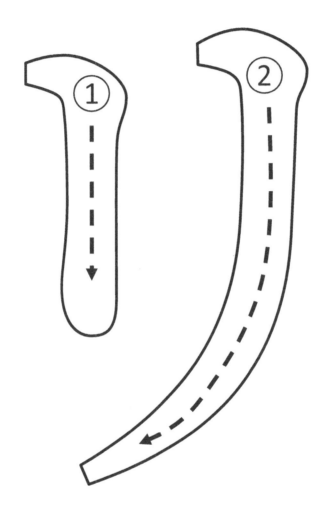

Should be pronounced « RI »

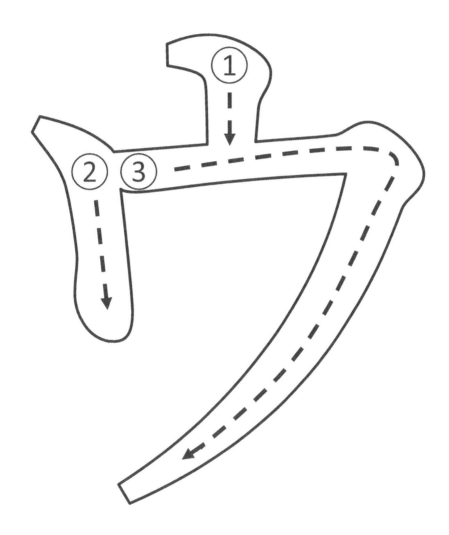

Should be pronounced « U »

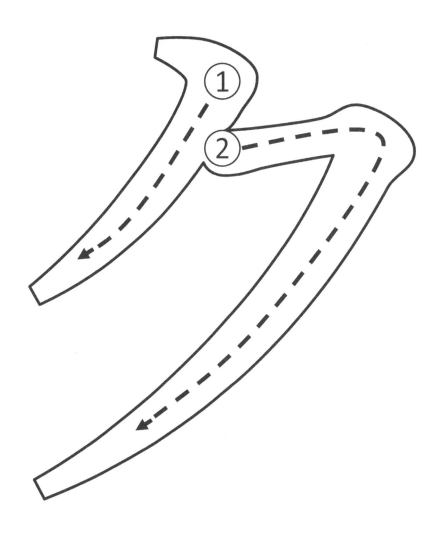

Should be pronounced « KU »

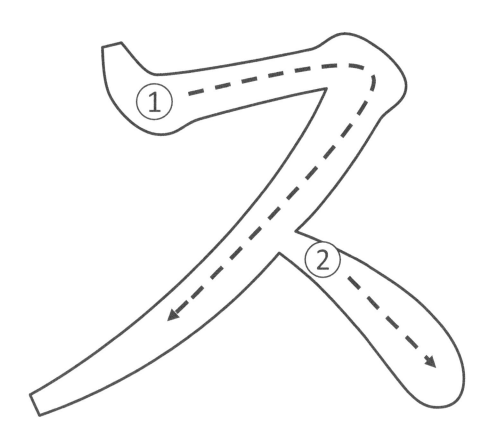

Should be pronounced « SU »

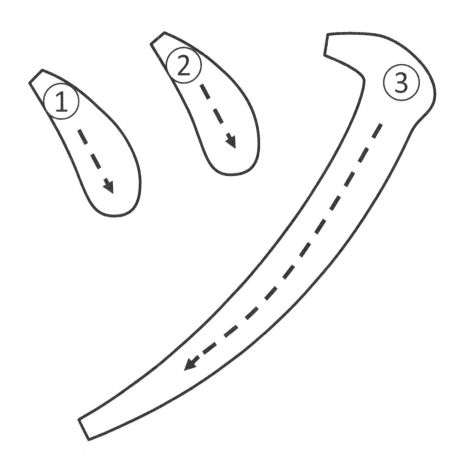

Should be pronounced « TSU »

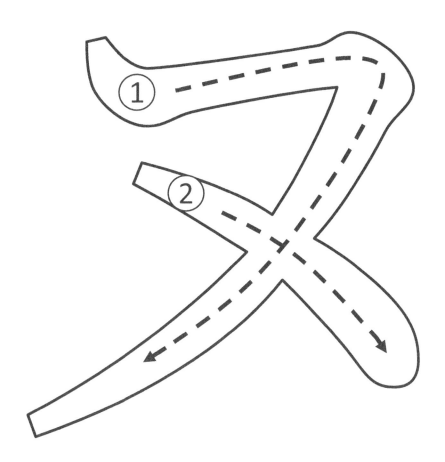

Should be pronounced « NU »

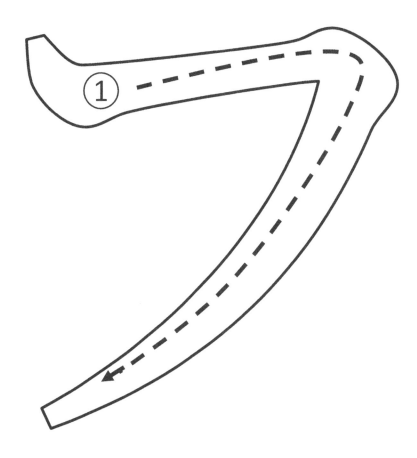

Should be pronounced « FU »

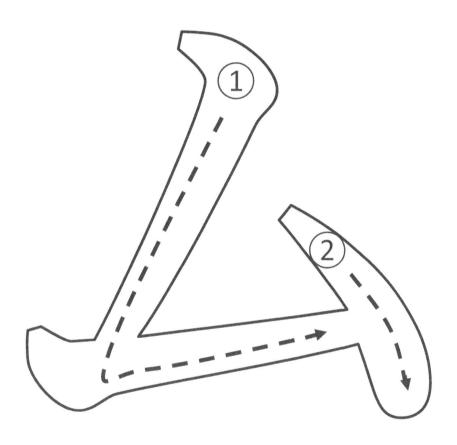

Should be pronounced « MU »

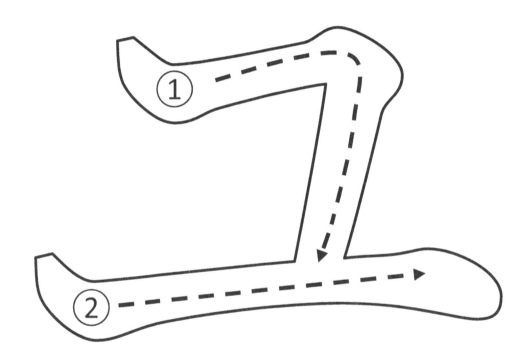

Should be pronounced « YU »

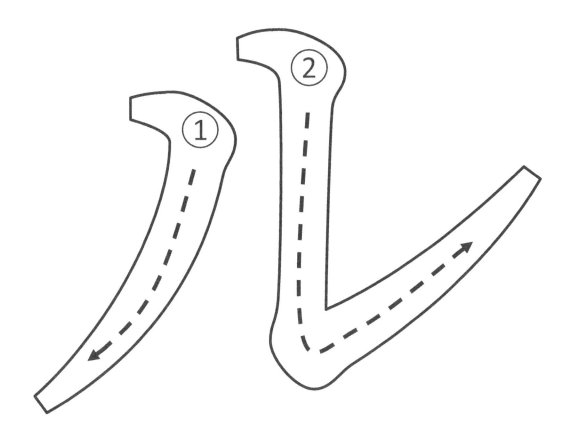

Should be pronounced « RU »

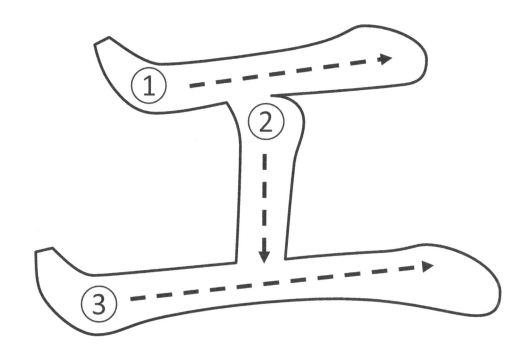

Should be pronounced « E »

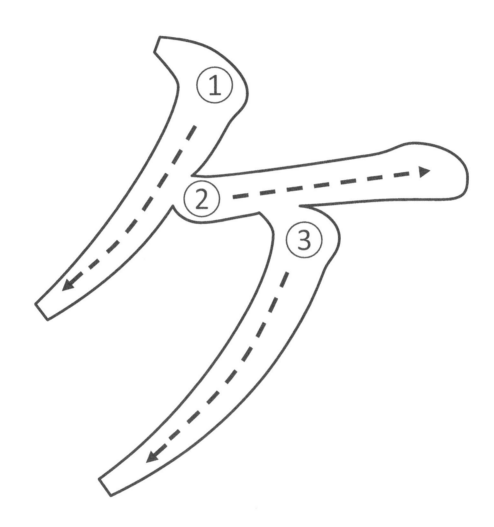

Should be pronounced « KE »

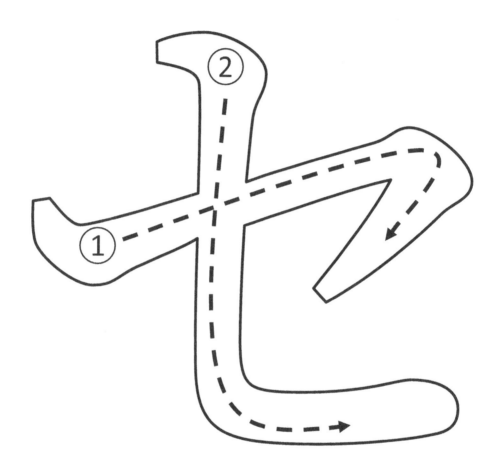

Should be pronounced « SE »

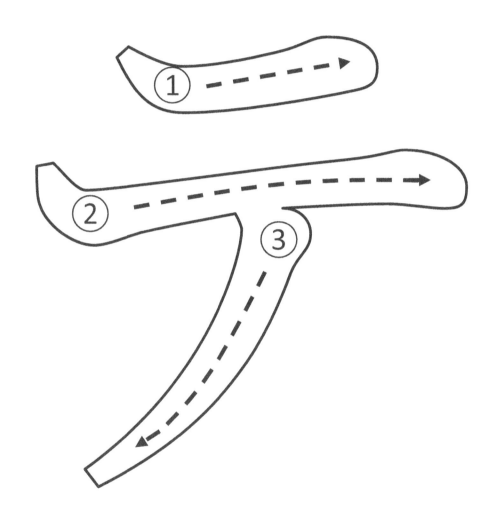

Should be pronounced « TE »

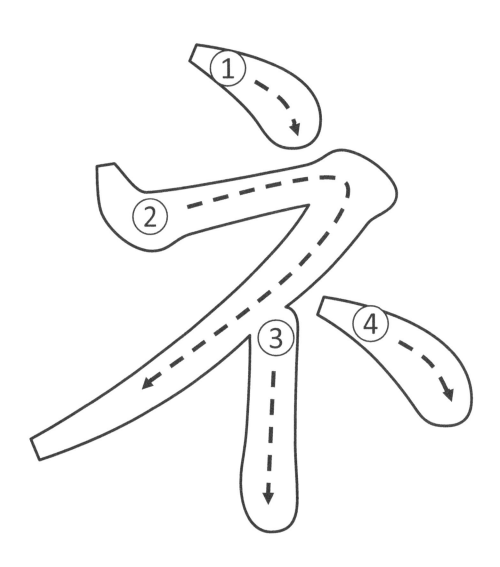

Should be pronounced « NE »

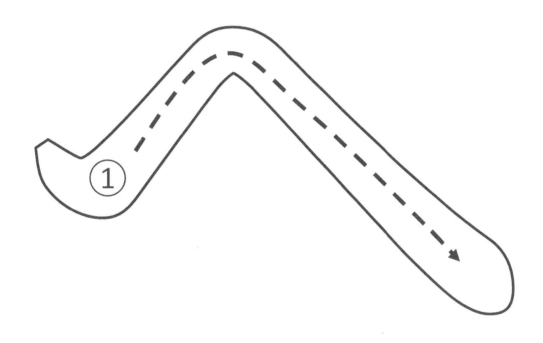

Should be pronounced « HE »

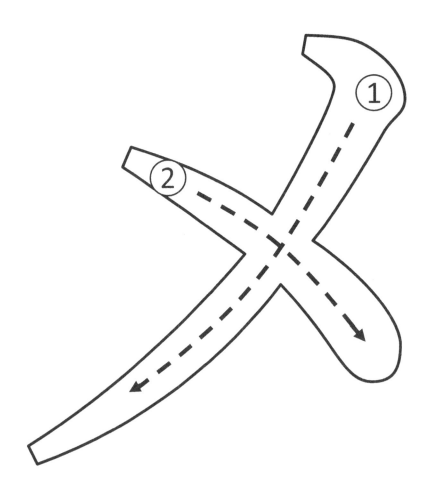

Should be pronounced « ME »

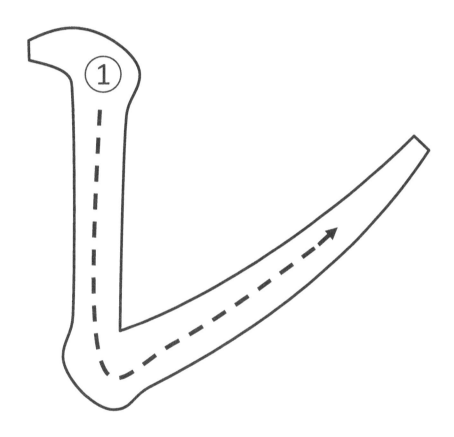

Should be pronounced « RE »

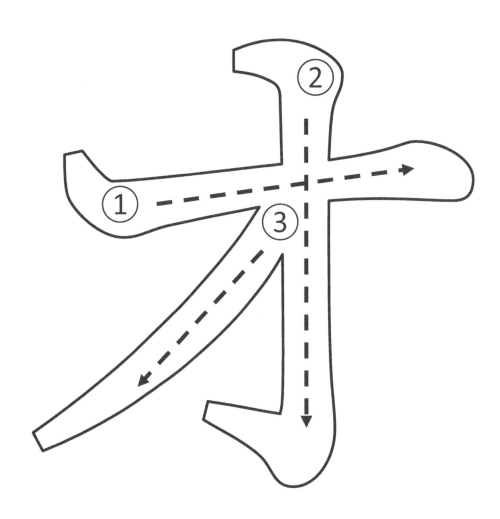

Should be pronounced « O »

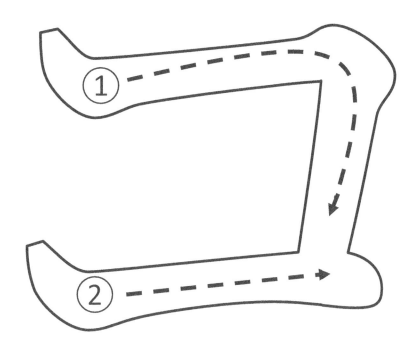

Should be pronounced « KO »

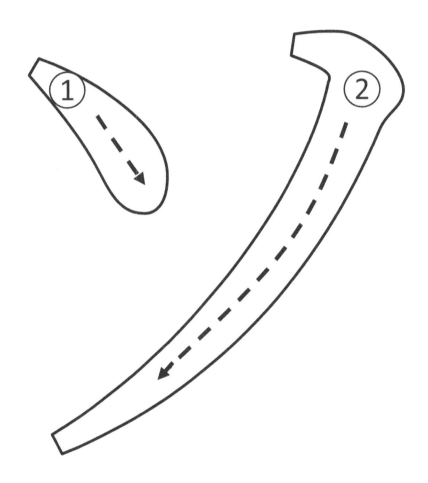

Should be pronounced « SO »

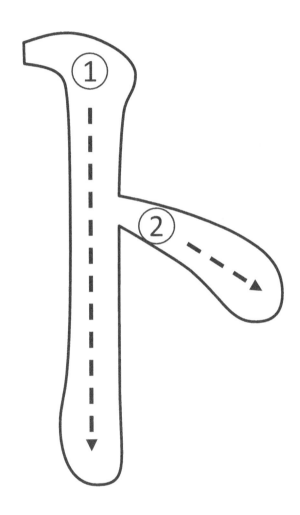

Should be pronounced « TO »

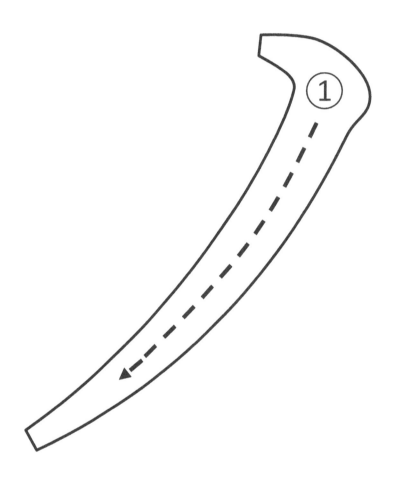

Should be pronounced « NO »

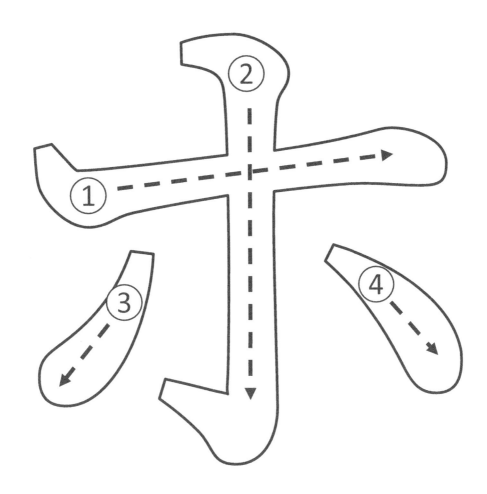

Should be pronounced « HO »

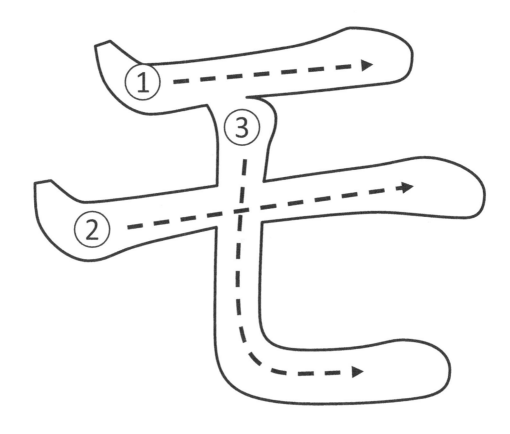

Should be pronounced « MO »

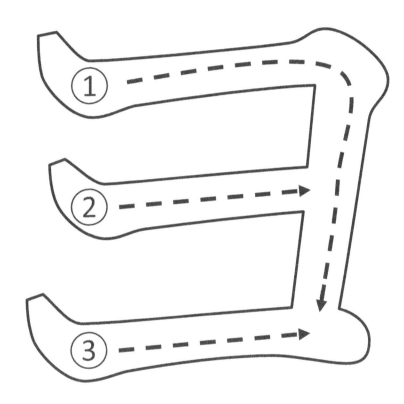

Should be pronounced « YO »

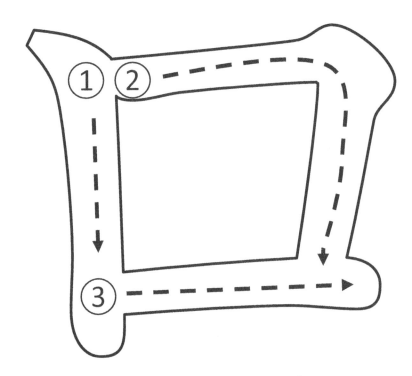

Should be pronounced « RO »

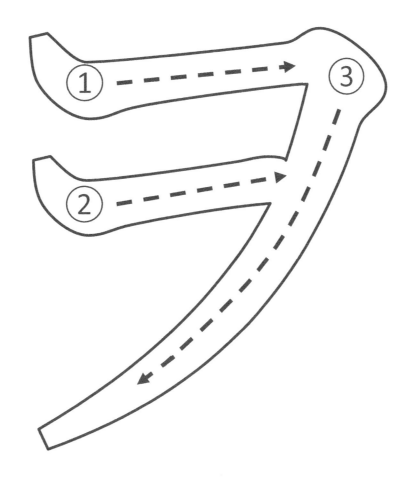

Should be pronounced « WO »

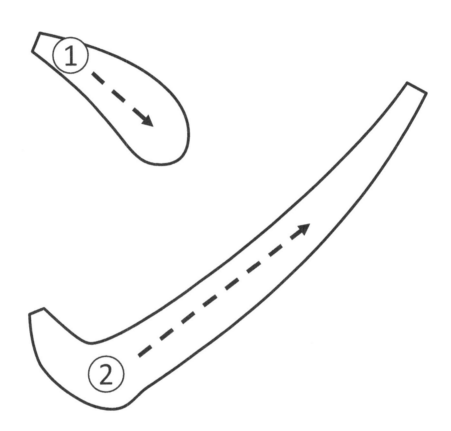

-N

KATAKANA
SMALLER CHARACTERS

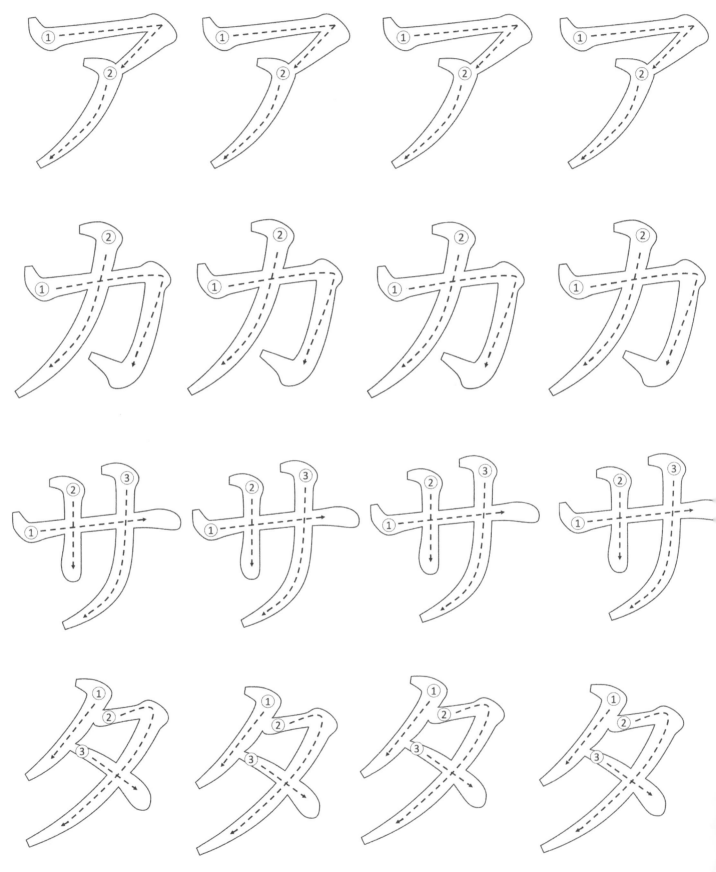

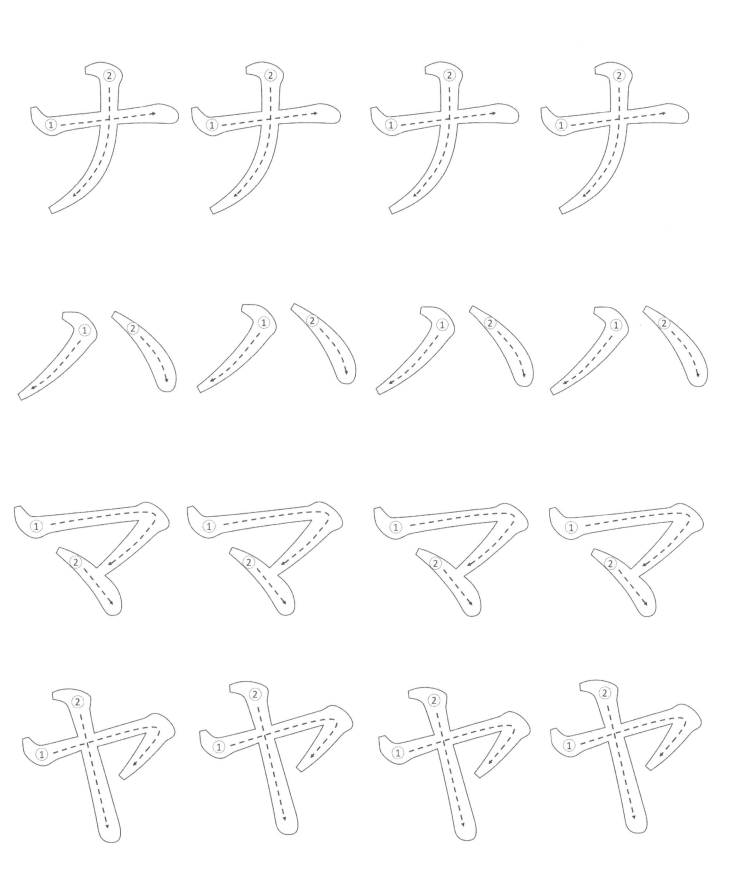

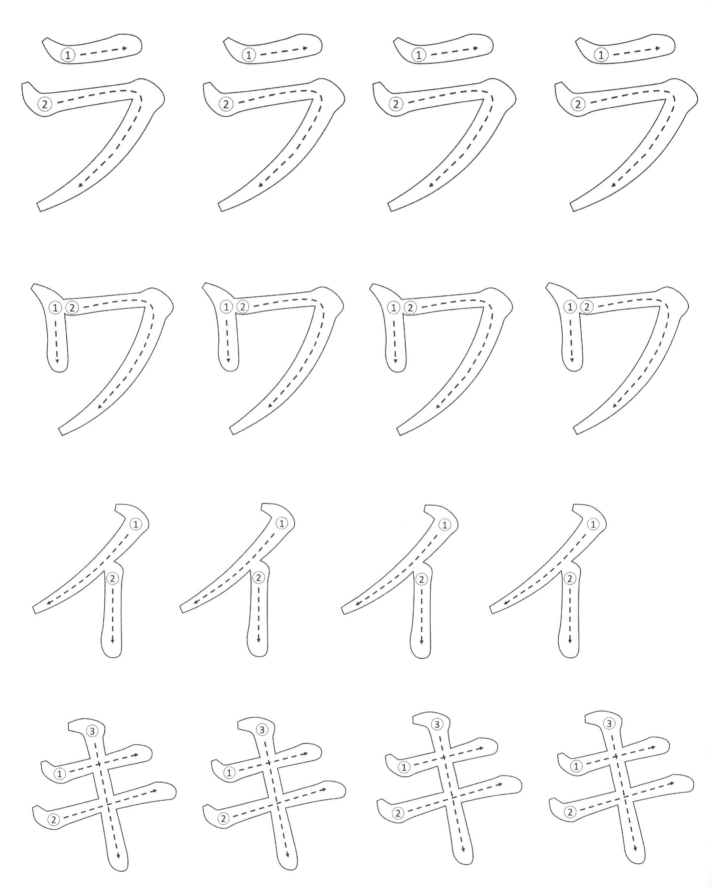

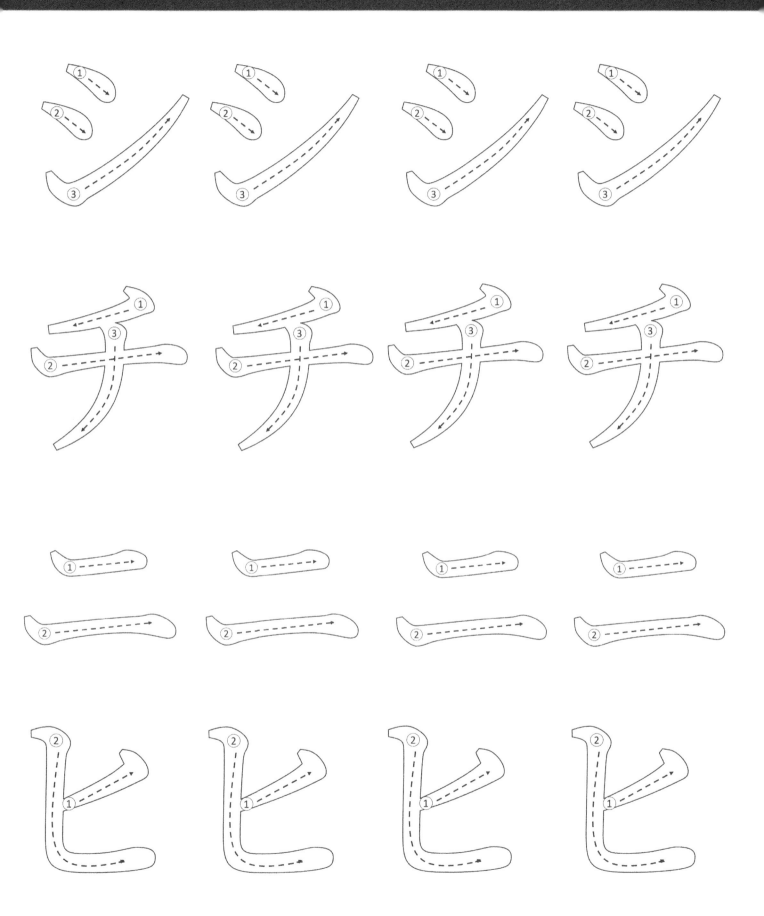

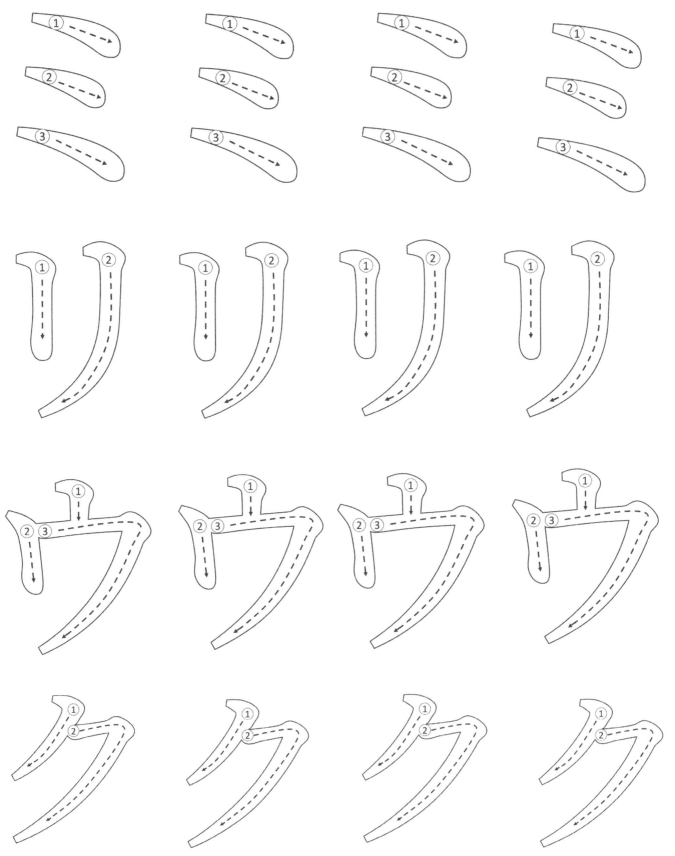

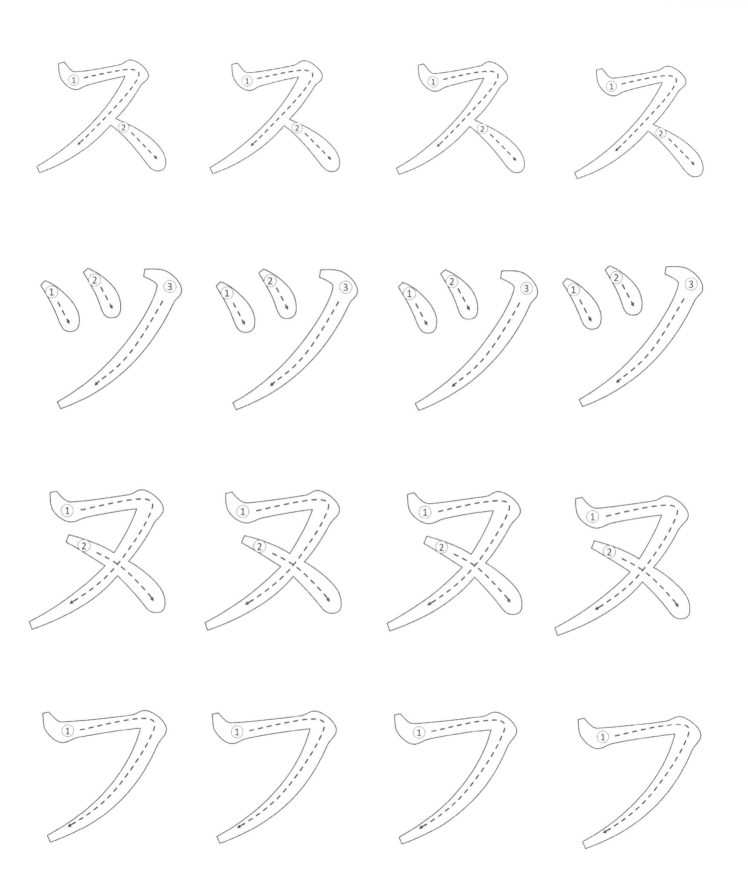

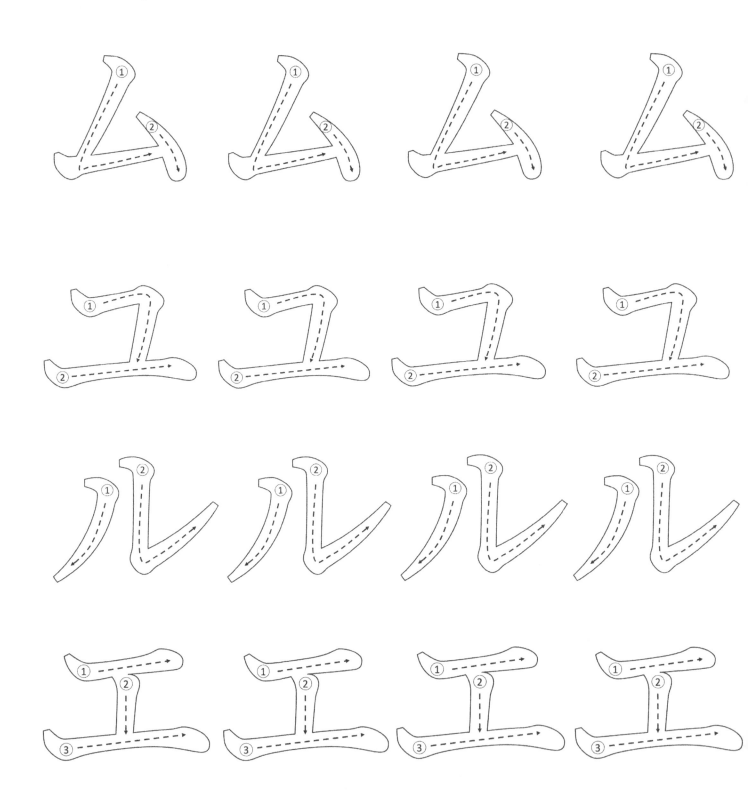

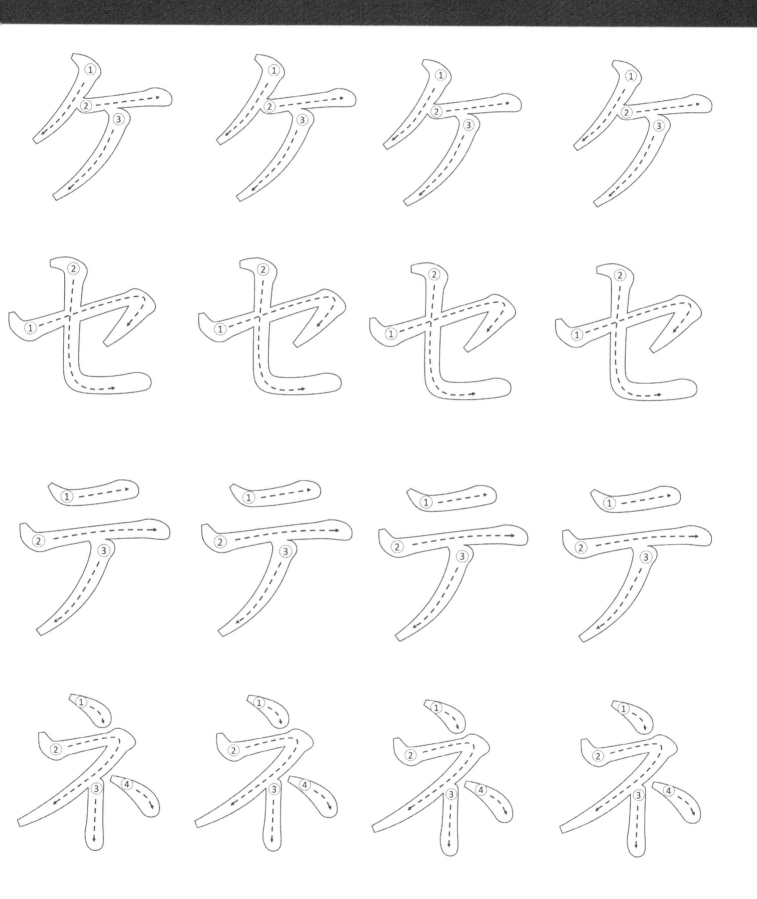

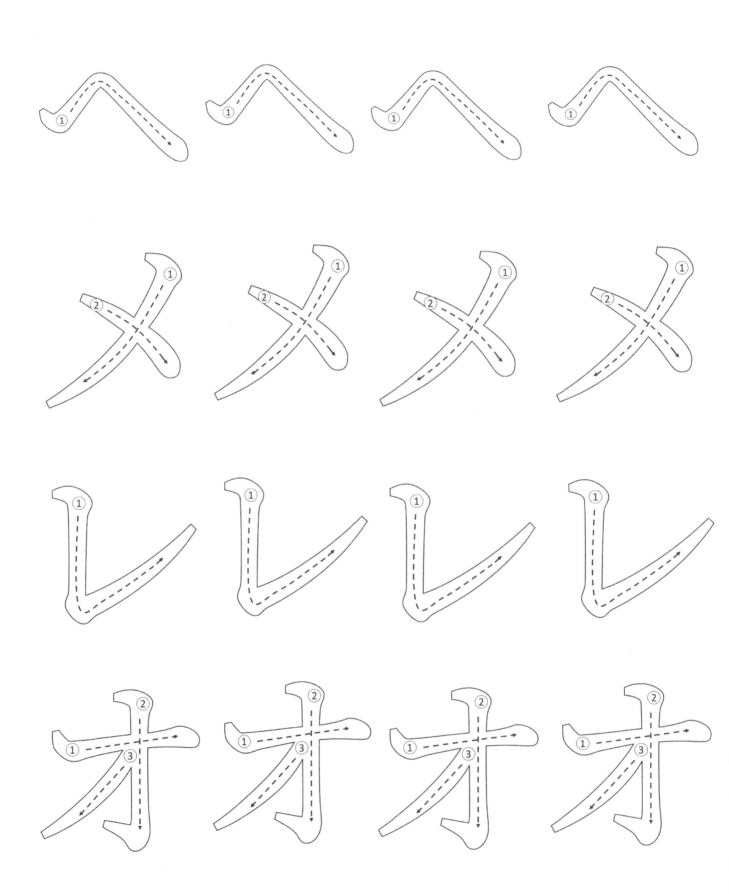

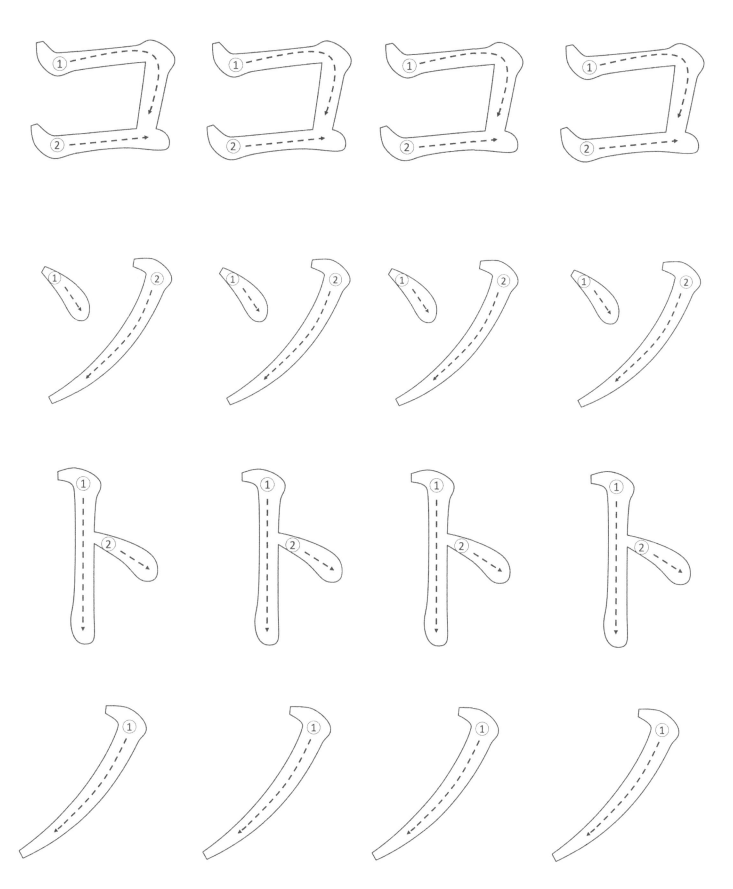

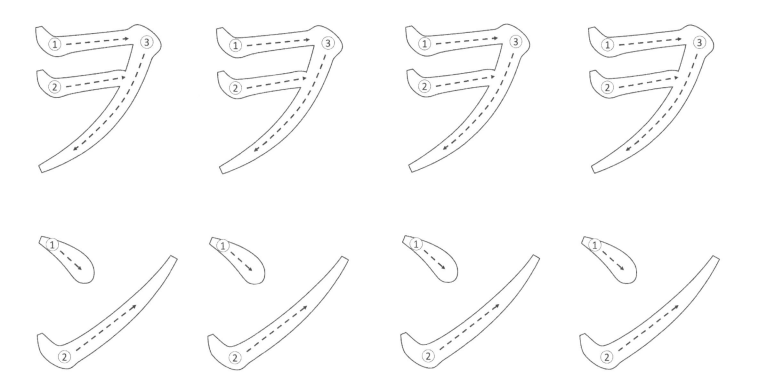

Made in the USA
Las Vegas, NV
05 November 2024